San Diego and Honolulu

A PhotoJournal through a Sailor's Eye

1920-1943

Petei McHenry

San Diego and Honolulu, A PhotoJournal through a Sailor's Eye, 1920-1943

By Petei McHenry

Published by:
    GP Marketing
    PO Box 1091
    Valley Center, CA 92082 U.S.A.
    760.749.0587

All rights reserved. No part of this book may be reproduced or transmitted in any form or by any means, electronic or mechanical, including photocopying, recording or by any information storage and retrieval system without written permission from the author, except for the inclusion of brief quotation in a review.

Although the author and publisher have exhaustively researched all sources to ensure the accuracy and completeness of the information contained in this book, we assume no responsibility for errors, omissions, or any inconsistency contained herein. Errors brought to the attention of the publisher and verified to the satisfaction of the publisher will be corrected in future editions.

All photographs are from the personal photograph collection of the author and the descendants of Ernest Joseph Crevier.

Copyright 2002 ; by Petei McHenry
First Edition
Printed in the United States of America by Vanard Lithographers, Inc., San Diego, California.

Publisher's Cataloging-in-Publication Data
McHenry, Petei.
    San Diego and Honolulu : a photoJournal through a
sailor's eye, 1920-1943 / Petei McHenry. — 1st ed.
    p. cm.
    Includes index.[[
    LCCN 99066637
    ISBN 0-9660789-2-6
    1. Navy-yards and naval stations—California—San
Diego—Pictorial works. 2. Navy-yards and naval
stations—Hawaii—Honolulu—Pictorial works. 3. San
Diego (Calif.)—History, Naval—Pictorial works.
4. Honolulu (Hawaii)—History, Naval—Pictorial works.
I. Title.

VA70.S36M34 2001   359.7'09794985'022
                        QBI01-201404

Acknowledgements

Although the photographs were taken from my grandfather's personal albums, this book could not have been produced without the generous help of many people. First, my thanks to those who helped determine the authenticity of the photographs at the San Diego Historical Society Archives; two fellow historians who helped identify the old ships, Bill Swank and Lt. Cmdr. Robert H. Dreher, USN Retired; also, my friends and comrades at the Valley Center Library who ordered special resource books and gave valuable advice and encouragment, Sandy Puccio and Pat Winneguth. Finally, I owe everything to my friends and family who not only helped research, edit, advise, and encourage, but allowed me the time and space to pursue this personal passion. My love to all.

Dedication

It is with great love and admiration that I dedicate this book to my mother, Erva "Peggy" Crevier Hardy, eldest daughter of Ernest Joseph Crevier. I wish they could have seen it in print.

Ernie and Erva, 1939

Table of Contents

Section I	San Diego, California: 1920-1943	8
Section II	Honolulu, Hawaii: 1942-1943	79
Index		146

Pictures tell the story...

The photographs in this book were found in my grandfather's old albums and are being published for the first time as a tribute to a young sailor alone in a new town with a camera as his constant companion.

In 1919, Ernest Joseph Crevier, left his parents' home in Massachusetts and hitchhiked his way to San Diego to join the United States Navy. He lied about his age in order to enlist because he was only seventeen years old at the time. He served as a Musician First Class at North Island after he purchased a used clarinet and taught himself to play using mail-order lessons. In about 1923, the band was transferred to the new San Diego Naval Training Center.

He fell in love with San Diego, married a local woman, and settled down. His four children were born there and after completing his tour of duty with the Navy, continued to live in San Diego. After conquering the clarinet, Ernie learned to play the saxophone and joined the Musician's Union to enable him to play with local bands and orchestras at various night spots in San Diego. He worked for Civil Service during the day in the "Paint and Dope" shop on North Island and during World War II, Ernie transferred to Honolulu, Hawaii where he worked from 1942 to 1943. Unfortunately, his family was unable to accompany him, but his love of photography continued during those Hawaiian years.

After returning to San Diego in 1943, Ernie received his Contractor's License to paint buildings and houses. One of the monumental tasks involved painting the San Diego County Administration Building on Pacific Highway during the 1950s. He loved new inventions and was one of the first on his block to purchase a new color television. His love of photography expanded with movie cameras and color photography. He lived in the small community of Hillcrest until his death in 1970 when his albums were discovered in an old trunk in his garage and seen by the family for the first time. When my grandmother, Ella May Crevier Shetler, showed me the albums, it became an important task to share these photos with others.

In order to retain the originality of the photographs, they have not been retouched or changed in any way other than digital scanning. Many of the photographs contained Ernie's handwritten captions, which made identification a simple task. Of those that were not captioned, research and documentation were attempted to the best of the author's ability. Errors brought to the attention of the publisher will be corrected in future printings.

San Diego, California

Section I
1920 - 1943

Sailors at the San Diego Mission de Alcala, ca. 1920

Horton Plaza, ca. 1920

Union Depot, 1920

Municipal Pier, 1920

The Harbor of the Sun, ca. 1920
[Named for a popular book written by Max Miller in the 1940s]

Destroyers at Santa Fe Dock at the Foot of Market Street, ca. 1920

U.S.S. Nevada or Oklahoma Battleship in San Diego Bay, ca. 1920

Oklahoma Class Battleship in San Diego Bay, ca. 1920

Battleships Moored in San Diego Bay, ca. 1920

A British Battleship in San Diego Bay, ca. 1920

General John J. Pershing in Balboa Park, 1923

Admiral Roger Welles Taking Command of the 11th Naval District, ca. 1920

Admiral Welles and Unidentified Official, ca. 1920

Captain Tombs, Admiral Welles, and Two Unidentified Officers, ca. 1920

Officers of U.S. Naval Air Station, North Island, 1922
Captain Tombs Commanding

Bugle and Drum Corps at the U.S. Naval Air Station, North Island, 1922

Lined Up on Plaza for Personnel Inspection
at U.S. Naval Air Station, North Island, 1922

Captain Tombs Inspecting Haircuts
at U.S. Naval Air Station, North Island, 1922

Personnel Inspection at U.S. Naval Air Station, North Island, 1922

HS-2-L, or F-Boats on North Island, 1922

Seaplane Crew at U.S. Naval Air Station,
North Island, 1922

Seaplane Crew in Wading Boots
U.S. Naval Air Station, North Island, 1922

Russell on a Float Plane at U.S. Naval Air Station,
North Island, 1922

Float Plane or F-Boat Taking-off in San Diego Bay, 1922

Jennies at U.S. Naval Air Station, North Island, 1922

JN6, or Jennies at U.S. Naval Air Station, North Island, ca. 1920

Pilots and Crew of a Jennie at
U.S. Naval Air Station, North Island, 1922

Bad Landing of a Jennie on North Island with Unidentified Persons, ca.1920

No One Hurt in this Crash on North Island, ca. 1920

Airplane Crash on Dutch Flats, Pilot of this Plane Died, ca.1920
[Dutch Flats now is where Marine Corp Recruit Depot,
Naval Training Center, and Lindbergh Field are Located.]

Airplane Crash on Dutch Flats,
Pilot of this Plane Lived to Tell the Story, ca. 1920

Airplane Crash on Dutch Flats
Showing Wing and Cause of Crash, ca. 1920

Landing Party for Airplane Crash on Dutch Flats, ca. 1920

Free Balloon Race on North Island, ca. 1920

Start of a Balloon Race on North Island
with Observation Balloon in Position, ca. 1920

Observation Balloon for Balloon Race
on North Island, ca. 1920

Carrier of Free Balloon,
North Island, ca. 1920

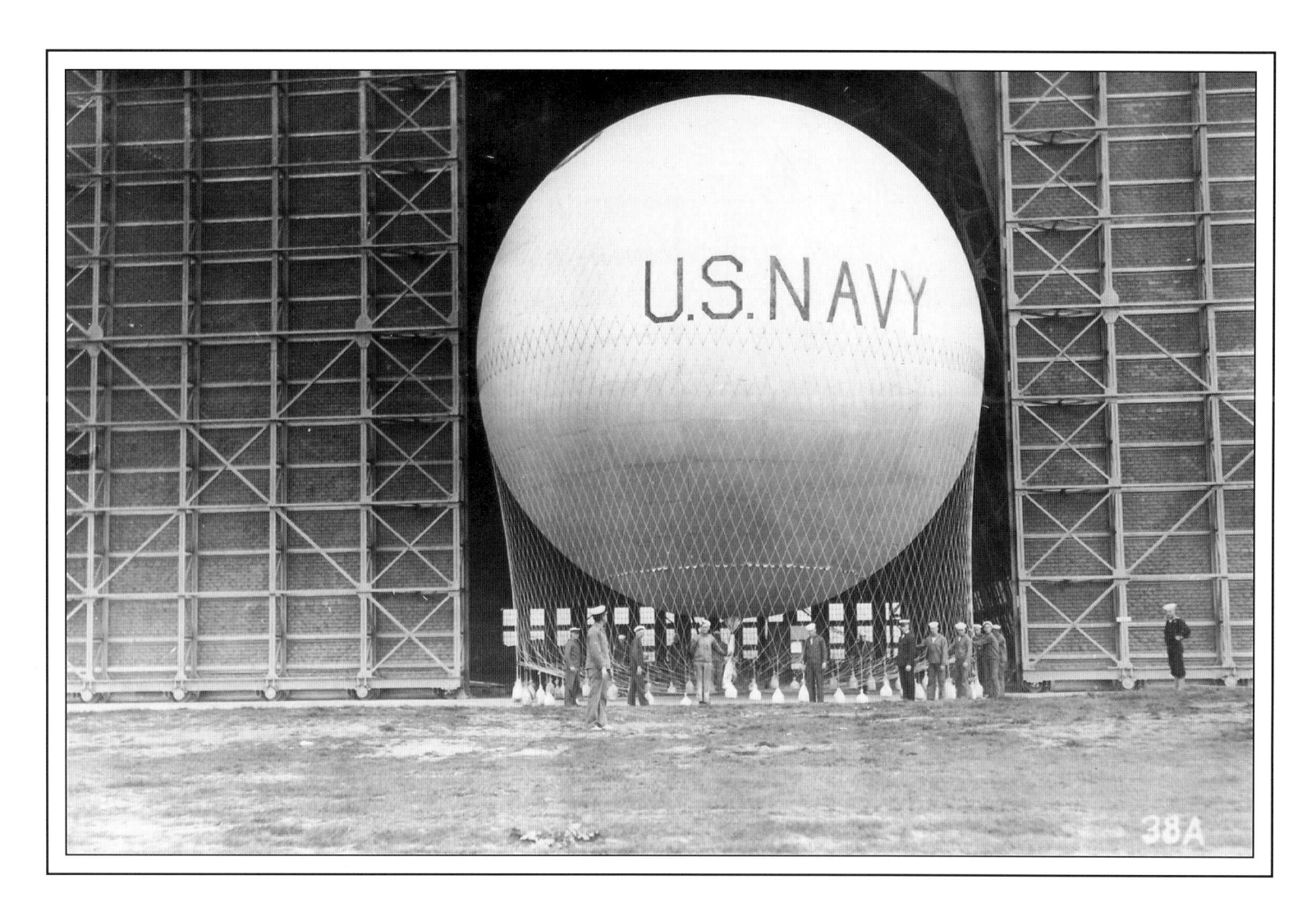

Free Balloon Held Down by Sandbags, North Island, ca. 1920

Free Balloon Lifting Off, North Island, ca. 1920

The Sky is the Limit, North Island, ca. 1920

Non-Rigid Dirigible, C-6, Leaving Hangar
North Island, ca. 1920

Ready to Start Motors of a C-6 Dirigible,
North Island, ca. 1920

C-6 Weighing Off Before Starting Motors,
North Island, ca. 1920

High-Hatting C-6 at North Island, ca. 1920

A Study in Profiles,
C-6 Dirigible Flying over North Island, ca. 1920

C-6 Dirigible Flying Over the Administration Building,
North Island, ca. 1920

Queen of the Sky in 1920,
C-6 at North Island

C-6 Getting Close to Earth,
North Island, ca. 1920

Happy Landing in the Hands of the Ground Crew of the C-6,
North Island, ca. 1920

C-6 Headed for the Barn, Stern First,
North Island, ca. 1920

C-6 Entering Hangar,
North Island, ca. 1920

B-18 Dirigible at Lakeside, July 4th, 1921

Liberty Party Lined up on the Old Dock Waiting for the "Nickel Snatcher" Ferry to North Island, Downtown San Diego, ca. 1920

Lined Up for Pay, North Island, 1920

Being Entertained by Scottish Highlanders at the Smoker,
North Island, 1920

Cross-Bay Swimming Meet, San Diego Bay, ca. 1920

Just a Little Home in the West, ca. 1920
[Possibly an Exhibition from the 1915 Panama-California Exposition in Balboa Park]

Left Photograph: Double Exposure Showing Ballard, E.J. Crevier, J.W. Stillwell, and Puppy on a Bridge Warning, ca. 1920; Second Photograph Shows a Burro Possibly a Tourist Shot from Tijuana, Mexico.
Right Photograph: E.J. Crevier and Old Truck, ca. 1920

Off-duty Sailors on a Trip to Cuyamaca,
December 1921

Left Photograph: E.J. Crevier and J.W. Stillwell, ca. 1920
Right Photograph: E.J. Crevier in Front of Building 102, North Island, ca. 1920

Left Photograph: E.J. Crevier and Pal, C. Erwin, ca. 1920
Right Photograph: U.S.N. Seaman E.J. Crevier in Friend's Army Uniform, ca. 1920

Members of the U.S. Naval Air Station Orchestra, North Island, ca. 1920
Top Left: Al Averell; Middle: Al Averell and E.J. Crevier; Right: C. Erwin and Al Averell
Bottom Left: C. Erwin; Right: C. Erwin and E.J. Crevier

U.S. Naval Air Station Orchestra, North Island, ca. 1920
Front Row Left to Right: D. Whitlatch, E.J. Crevier, P.J. Crueller, R.S. Click, C.W. Cleaver, M.J. McIntyre, P. Bixby, A.J. Englebrecht, L.J. Lewis, C. Willmar, E.E. McLain
Back Row: J.W. Stillwell, A. Dorashinski, R.B. Lawson, W.H. Moorhead, L.D. Smith, J.I. Woolsey, Ted Mullen, G.W. Berry, H. Buehler, C. Erwin, H.P. Joslynn, W. Green

U.S. Naval Air Station Orchestra, Naval Training Center, 1923
Left to Right: Newhall, McLain, Roseman, Dorashinski, Crevier, Averell, Pregg, Donavan, McIntyre

WPA Band at the Spreckel's Organ Pavilion Balboa Park, ca. 1930

Val Dage and the Ambassadors Band at Unidentified Location, ca. 1930s
[E. J. Crevier is First Person in the second Row from the right]

Ernie Crevier Playing the Saxophone with Unidentified Band
at the Gay '90s Nightclub, Downtown San Diego, ca. 1940s

Evelyn Reeser's Serenaders, Silverado Ballroom 1943
Ernie Crevier on the Sax, Evelyn Reeser on Piano, William "Bud" Basom with his string bass,
Gail Glancy on the violin, and Harold Weber on drums

Section II
1942 - 43

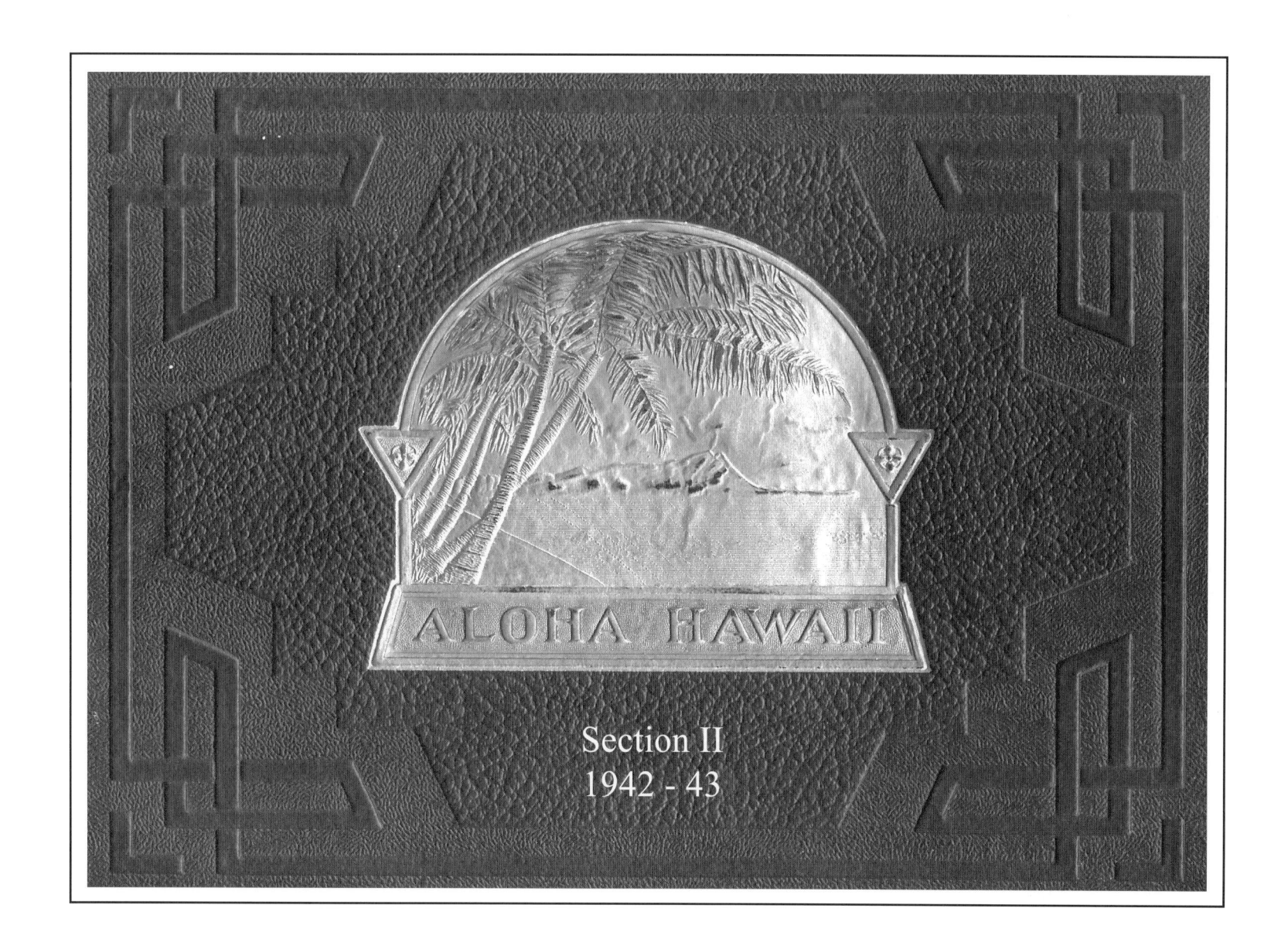

U.S.S. Lexington and U.S.S. Saratoga Outside Pearl Harbor, 1942
[Original taken from Christmas Eve dinner menu, U.S. Naval Officers Club, Honolulu]

Aloha, Arriving in Honolulu, 1942

Traditional Lei Maker, Honolulu, 1942

E.J. Crevier with Lei Maker, Honolulu, 1942

E.J. Crevier with Freshly Made Lei, Honolulu, 1942

Crossroads of the Pacific, Honolulu, 1942

E.J. Crevier at the Crossroads, Honolulu, 1942

E.J. Crevier on Motorcycle at the Crossroads,
Honolulu, 1942

Honolulu Recreation Center, 1942

Downtown Honolulu, 1943

King Kamehameha Statue, 1942

King Kamehameha Statue in Front of Iolani Palace, 1942

Iolani Palace, 1942
[Currently used as the State Office Building]

E.J. Crevier in Front of Hawaiian Things Shop, 1942

E.J. Crevier with Tiki, 1942

Waikiki Theater, 1942

Old Federal Building, Honolulu, 1942
[Currently the Main Post Office Building]

Old Army and Navy Young Men's Association Building, Honolulu, 1942
[Currently used for State offices]

Honolulu *Hale*, or City Hall, 1942

Royal Hawaiian Hotel, Waikiki Beach, 1942

Waikiki Beach with Diamond Head in Distance, 1942

Royal Hawaiian Island Band, 1943

Waikiki Beach Scene, 1943

View of the Royal Hawaiian Hotel, Waikiki Beach, 1943

Traditional Outrigger Canoes on Waikiki Beach, 1943

Polynesian Entertainers, 1943

Hula Lessons, 1943

Fresh Hawaiian Crabs for Sale, 1943

Joe Kaufman and Scotty Thompson in Front
of the Waikiki Curio Shop, Honolulu, 1943

Scotty Thompson and E.J. Crevier on Waikiki Beach
with the Royal Hawaiian and Moana Hotels in Background, 1943

Old Banyon Tree, Honolulu, 1943

Flowering Royal Poinciana Tree, Honolulu, 1943

Blossoming Euphorbia Plant, Honolulu, 1943

Bananas on the Tree, Honolulu, 1943

Fresh Fruit, Honolulu, 1943

Ship in the Harbor, Honolulu, 1943

Cruise Ship Lurline Coming into Port, Honolulu, 1943

Swimmers in the Harbor, Honolulu, 1943

Swim Meet, Honolulu, 1943

Buddies on Motorcycles, Honolulu, 1943

Main Street, Honolulu Cantonment, 1943

Recreation Hall, Honolulu Cantonment, 1943

U.S. Post Office, Honolulu Cantonment, 1943

Civil Service Police Station, Honolulu Cantonment, 1943

Damon Tract Grocery, Honolulu Cantonment, 1943

Waiting in Line for Monthly Rations, Honolulu Cantonment, 1943

E.J. Crevier at the Gas Alarm, Honolulu Cantonment, 1943

Barracks at Honolulu Cantonment, 1943

Navy Housing, Honolulu Cantonment, 1943

Supply Train Arriving at Honolulu Cantonment, 1943

Supply Train Fire, Honolulu Cantonment, 1943

Supply Train Wreck and Fire, Honolulu Cantonment, 1943

Transport Vehicles, Honolulu Cantonment, 1943

Tractor-pulled Transport, Honolulu Cantonment, 1943

Bus Trip to the Mountains of Oahu, 1943

Nu'uahu Pali Road, Oahu, 1943

Water Hole, Oahu, 1943

Water Falls, Oahu, 1943

Hawaiian Temple, Laie, Oahu, 1943

Pineapple Field, Oahu, 1943

Traditional Ox and Plow Farming with Inexperienced Helper, Oahu, 1943

Blow Hole, Oahu, 1943

Crashing Waves, Oahu, 1943

Aloha, Hawaii, Oahu Sunset, 1943

RULES AND SUGGESTIONS FOR PHOTOGRAPHY IN WAR-TIME HAWAII

A reprint of General Orders Number 60 and hints as to the authorized and legal use of your camera.

"Photographs of subjects not of military or naval significance nor specifically forbidden by government regulations will be released by the Office of Censorship."

Lt. Col. Harold R. Shaw
District Postal Censor.

Hawaii presents many breath-taking picture opportunities that are not affected by restrictions. Kodak Hawaii, Ltd., suggests that you abide by the regulations and remember that the best pictures are made on Eastman Film.

KODAK HAWAII, LTD.
P. O. Box 1260   Honolulu, T. H.

GENERAL ORDER No. 60

SECTION 1. RESTRICTIONS ON PHOTOGRAPHY.—
1. Cameras. a. As published in General Orders No. 32, Office of the Military Governor, 18 December 1941, enemy aliens are prohibited from having in their possession or having the use of any camera at any time.
   b. The use of cameras by persons other than enemy aliens is hereby prohibited as follows:
   (1) Cameras will not be used on any beach in the Territory of Hawaii.
   (2) Cameras will not be used while in or on any plane, boat or ship in waters or air abounding the Territory of Hawaii.
2. Photographs—a. Photographs may be taken for commercial and personal use, but in no instance will photographs be taken of the following subjects:
   (1) Any military or naval reservation, post, arsenal, proving ground, range, camp, fort, yard, station, district or area.
   (2) Any shore line within the Territory of Hawaii.
   (3) Any military or naval installations, equipment, aircraft, weapons, ammunition, vehicles, ships, vessels, instruments, engines, manufacturing machinery, tools, devices, or any other equipment whatsoever in the possession of the Army or Navy, or in the course of experimentation, development, manufacture for delivery to the Army or Navy.
   b. Exceptions to the above restrictions are limited to those persons duly authorized by competent military or naval authorities.
By order of the Military Governor:
(Signed)   THOMAS H. GREEN,
Colonel, J. A. G. D., Executive.
Office of Military Governor

UNRESTRICTED SUBJECTS

Animals—farm, zoo, and at home
Bathers (except on beaches)
Cathedrals and Churches
Hawaiian Building and Statues
Indoor subjects—portraits and table top-set-ups
Industrial Scenes (except war-work)
Men and Officers in uniform
Architectural subjects
Cloud formations

Babies and Children	Birds
Cyclists	Groups
Farm subjects	Homes
Family Groups	Models
Figure studies	Nature Studies
Fish	Oddities
Flowers	Park Scenes
Flowering Trees	Portraits (outdoor)
Games	Sports
Gardens	Sunsets

DON'T CONCEAL YOUR CAMERA. One of the best ways to avoid trouble is to keep your camera in plain sight at all times. Do not carry it into restricted areas.

CARRY IDENTIFICATION. Always be sure and have plenty of identification on your person.

WHEN IN DOUBT do not take a picture but consult the authorities first.

Rules and Suggestions for War-Time Photography, 1943
[Note how closely these suggestions were followed in the preceding pages]

Index

Symbols

11th Naval District
    Admiral Roger Welles 21

A

Admiral Roger Welles 22
Admiral Welles 23

B

B-18 Dirigible
    Lakeside 61

C

Captain Tombs 23
Cuyamaca Trip 68

E

Evelyn Reeser's Serenaders 77

H

Hawaiian Crabs 107
Honolulu 81, 96
    Banana Tree 113
    Banyon Tree 110
    Downtown Overview 89
    Euphorbia Plant 112
    Fresh Fruit 114
    Harbor 115
        Cruise Ship Lurline 116
    Hawaiian Things Shop 93
    Iolani Palace 92
    Lei Maker 82, 83
    Leis 84
    Motorcycles 119
    Pacific Crossroads 85, 86
    Recreation Center 88
    Royal Poinciana Tree 111
    Swim Meet 118
    Swimmers in the Harbor 117
    Tiki 94
    Waikiki Theater 95
    YMCA Building 97
Honolulu Cantonment
    Barracks 127
    Civil Service Police Station 123
    Damon Tract Grocery 124
    Gas alarm 126
    Housing 128
    Main Street 120
    Rations 125
    Recreation Hall 121
    Transportation
        Military vehicles 132
        Tractor-pulled 133
        Train 129
        Train fire 130
        Train wreck 131
    U.S. Post Office 122
Hula Lessons 106

N

Naval Training Center
    U.S. Naval Air Station Orchestra 73
North Island
    Airplane Crash 37, 38

Balloon Race 44
C-6 Dirigible
    51, 52, 53, 54, 55, 56, 57, 58, 59, 60
Drum and Bugle Corps 25
Free Balloon 46, 47, 48, 49
Free Balloon Race 43
Housing
    Tennis players 69
HS-2-L or F-boats 29
Non-Rigid Dirigible 50
Observation Balloon 45
Sailors 63
Scottish Highlanders 64
U.S. Naval Air Station 24, 26, 27, 28, 30, 31, 32
    Jennie (JN6) 36
    Jennies (JN6) 34, 35
U.S. Naval Air Station Orchestra 71, 72

O

Oahu
    Blow Hole 141
    Farming
        Ox and Plow 140
    Laie
        Hawaiian Temple 138
    Mountains 134
    Nu'uahu Pali Road 135
    Pacific Ocean 142
    Pineapple field 139
    Sunset 143
    Water falls 137
    Water hole 136

P

Panama-California Exposition
   House in the West 66
Pearl Harbor
   U.S.S. Lexington, U.S.S. Saratoga 80
Polynesian Entertainers 105

R

Royal Hawaiian Hotel
   Waikiki Beach 103
Royal Hawaiian Island Band 101

S

San Diego
   Balboa Park
      General John J. Pershing 20
   Battleships 18
   British Battleship 19
   Dutch Flats
      Airplane Crash 39, 40, 41
      Landing Party 42
   Gay '90s Nightclub 76
   Harbor of the Sun 14
   Horton Plaza 11
   Mission de Alcala 10
   Municipal Pier 13
   Oklahoma Class Battleship 17
   Santa Fe Dock
      Destroyers 15
   U.S.S. Nevada or Oklahoma
      Battleship 16
   Union Depot 12

San Diego Bay
   Cross-bay Swim Meet 65
   Float Plane 33
Sunset 143

V

Val Dage and the Ambassadors Band 75

W

Waikiki Beach 102
   Diamond Head 100
   Royal Hawaiian Hotel 99
Waikiki Curio Shop 108
War-time Photography
   Photographer's Rules 144